STUDY GUIDE

FOUR SESSIONS

TOO BUSY
NOT
TO PRAY

Slowing Down to Be with God

BILL HYBELS
WITH ASHLEY WIERSMA

ZONDERVAN®

WILLOW
Willow Creek Resources

ZONDERVAN.com/
AUTHORTRACKER
follow your favorite authors

ZONDERVAN

Too Busy Not to Pray Study Guide
Copyright © 2013 by Bill Hybels

This title is also available as a Zondervan ebook. Visit www.zondervan.com/ebooks.

Requests for information should be addressed to:
Zondervan, Grand Rapids, Michigan 49530

ISBN 978-0-310-69491-5

Based on *Too Busy Not to Pray* by Bill Hybels, © 1988, 1998, 2008 by Bill Hybels.
Used by permission of InterVarsity Press, P.O. Box 1400, Downers Grove, IL 60515,
USA. www.ivpress.com

Cover design: Ron Huizinga
Cover photography: Getty Images / Ryan McVay; Masterfile
Interior design: Matthew Van Zomeren

Printed in the United States of America

15 16 17 18 19 20 /QG/ 20 19 18 17 16 15 14 13 12 11 10 9 8 7 6 5 4 3 2 1

CONTENTS

A NOTE FROM BILL HYBELS

Nearly twenty-five years ago, I slid into a season of disheartening prayerlessness. Despite the fact that I wanted to pray, I needed to pray, and I knew that as a pastor and a Christ follower I *should* pray, I did not pray. Sure, I prayed before meals with my family. I prayed from the platform before and after sermons I preached. But in my private life, in my daily life, in my heart of hearts, prayer wasn't part of the deal.

The book *Too Busy Not to Pray* was a prayerless man's attempt to recharge his prayer life, and that prayerless man was me. I figured if I went through the paces of writing a book on prayer—studying every Bible verse on prayer, researching other books on prayer, and talking to people about the prayer practices that helped them stay out of a rut—then surely my dreaded season of prayerlessness would come to an end. Furthermore, I reasoned that if God decided to bless the book, maybe other people's prayer lives would be resuscitated too. Suffice it to say, I've been writing books for three decades, and no book of mine has outpaced *Too Busy* in terms of number of units sold. Only God.

Recently I was compelled to capture my best thinking on the subject of prayer, the result of which you hold in your hands. I put together these four sessions to convey a single idea: *you can become a person of prayer.* Even if you've never prayed before. Even if you're in a prayerless place yourself. You can learn to pray. You—with your upbringing, with your knowledge, with your values system, with your quirks and foibles and fears—*you* can be a person of prayer, someone who talks to and listens to God. You don't have to go back to school or go on a diet, you don't have to get older or get richer or get wiser, you don't have to be better or be stronger or be anything, *anyone*, other than who you are right now, today. To be a person of prayer, all you have to do is decide. Decide that prayer matters. Decide that *your* prayers matter. Decide that there really is a God who is willing and able to help you in your time of need. And then slow down, look up, and *pray*.

A life led by God is the richest life there is, and if you'll stick with me for these four sessions, I think you'll come away convinced that this is the life for you.

Ready to find out if I'm right?

Throughout the guide, you'll find boxed content to reinforce the themes you're exploring in each session. Except for Scripture passages, which are marked accordingly, all quotes are taken from the 2008 version of my book *Too Busy Not to Pray*.

WHY PRAY?

Through the ages, prayer has changed attitudes, changed circumstances, changed minds, delivered wisdom, delivered resources, delivered deliverance, cured sickness, calmed winds, healed marriages, untangled financial knots, emboldened the oppressed, expanded the gates of heaven, and brought to life those who were dead. In a word, prayer has mattered. And evidently, we believe it still does. Three out of four people claim to pray every single day, which means that in spite of our sometimes-fragile faith, we keep coming back to the ideas that God is willing to hear us when we call, and that he is able to lend a helping hand.

In short, this is why we pray.

SUGGESTED READING

Prior to meeting with your group to discuss session 1, read the following chapters of the book *Too Busy Not to Pray* (2008 edition):

Chapter 1, "God of Peace, God of Power"
Chapter 2, "God Is Willing"
Chapter 3, "God Is Able"

INTRODUCTION

In functional families, children learn from the earliest of ages that their mother and father will respond to them when they have a pressing need. As babies, they know that when they cry in the middle of the night, Mom will show up with a concerned look on her face, eager to help sort out whether food or cuddles or added warmth is going to solve the problem—and then help provide that resource as quickly as possible.

They know that when Dad reaches down to pick them up, there will be gentleness in his touch. They know that when they spit up, Mom will be there to patiently clean up the mess. They know that when they smile, loved ones will smile back.

As they get older, they come to understand that birthdays and Christmastime will always involve meaningful traditions and lots of love. They understand that rules are established for their protection. They understand that when they violate those rules, there may be consequences, but also there will be forgiveness, there will be grace. They understand that whatever else happens, there *always* will be love. This is how it goes with good parents; they never neglect trying to meet real needs, and they never neglect trying to love well.

In Matthew 7, we read some pretty powerful words from Jesus about how we are to approach our heavenly Father in prayer. "Don't bargain with God," he instructs. "Be direct. Ask for what you need. This isn't a cat-and-mouse, hide-and-seek game we're in. If your child asks for bread, do you trick him with sawdust? If he asks for fish, do you scare him with a live snake on his plate? As bad as you are, you wouldn't think of such a thing. You're at least decent to your own children. So don't you think the God who conceived you in love will be even better?" (vv. 7–11 MSG).

What he's saying, essentially, is this: As human parents, the best we can do is still not so good, when compared with God's goodness. We are fallen. We are fearful. We are broken. We are self-centered and sin-scarred and weak. Yes, we do our level best to love our kids well, but we are imperfect and inconsistent and our motives are impure at times. But not so with God.

No, we can come boldly before his throne, knowing that while earthly parents try to meet needs, our heavenly Father is *always* willing, *always* able to do so. While earthly parents try to love well, our heavenly Father loves us with a *perfect and everlasting* love.

CONVERSATION STARTER

We may shake our heads and chuckle at the kid who hands his teacher his completed geography test and then prays, "God, please make Detroit the capital of Michigan," but most of us have offered up our share of misdirected prayers from time to time.

For example, we fly down neighborhood streets, late to church again, praying that we won't get pulled over. We pray that our first date with this self-absorbed person soon will be over. We pull into a parking spot designated for drivers with disabilities, praying as we dash into the store that nobody who really needs the slot will be left circling the lot the entire time we're inside. When our kids are small, we pray they won't wake from a nap while we're trying to see just *one task* through to completion. We pray the snowstorm that's making a beeline for our town will miraculously be diverted, so we can carry on with carefully crafted plans. Women, in particular, pray that their "skinny clothes" will somehow still fit.

What is a humorous prayer request you've made along the way? Did things pan out the way you hoped they would? Share your thoughts with your group.

VIDEO NOTES

As you watch the video for session 1, use the following outline to record anything that stands out to you.

Prayer, through the ages

First experiences with prayer

Prayer that stirs the soul

The season of prayerlessness

A deep dive into Scriptures on prayer

God's inclination toward kindness

VIDEO DISCUSSION AND BIBLE STUDY

1. Bill cited many results that prayer has yielded throughout history, including that it has changed attitudes and changed circumstances, delivered wisdom and delivered peace, and more. What are a few simple, practical things that you have seen prayer do firsthand?

2. The first time Bill experienced prayer was in the church of his youth. Thinking back on your own spiritual history, what was your first experience with prayer like, and where did it occur? How did that early experience shape your understanding of prayer and of God?

3. If you were to divide your prayer life into seasons or eras, what word or phrase would you use in naming each of them? For Bill, one prayer season was marked by *disillusionment*. Another, during his camp-counselor days, was marked by sheer *exhilaration*. A third was marked by *prayerlessness*. Take ninety seconds to note on the following grid a one- or

> When we work, *we* work, but when we pray, *God* works.

two-word description of your own "prayer eras" as well as the situations or circumstances that surrounded them, and then share an entry or two with your group. An example is offered.

MY PRAYER ERAS	
Descriptor	**Circumstances Surrounding This Era**
Ex.: Authenticity	I was a new believer and was humbled that the God who created me—who created everything—was eager to have a relationship with me. I prayed all the time, and about everything, it seemed.

4. Based on the eras of prayer you recorded on the grid in question 3, what is the closest you've ever come to experiencing a season of "prayerlessness," similar to the one Bill described? Below, list three to five characteristics that describe what it feels like to live without the priority of prayer.

•

•

•

•

•

5. What situations, frustrations, or questions do you suppose typically cause people who love God to stop communicating with him through prayer?

6. Philippians 4:6 says to not "be anxious about *anything*, but in *every* situation, by prayer and petition, with thanksgiving, present your requests to God" (emphasis added). Given that most everyone has experienced ups and downs, highs and lows, and ebbs and flows to his or her prayer life, do you think it's actually possible to live this way? Why or why not?

7. For Bill, the solution to reconnecting with God after a time of prayerlessness was doing a deep dive into Scriptures dealing with the topic of prayer. Both in the video and in chapter 1 of the book, he cites several of the verses he found impactful, including the following:

> The LORD is near to all who call on him, to all who call on him in truth. (Psalm 145:18)

> "Ask and it will be given to you; seek and you will find; knock and the door will be opened to you." (Matthew 7:7)

> Taste and see that the LORD is good; blessed is the one who takes refuge in him. (Psalm 34:8)

> I waited patiently for the LORD; he turned to me and heard my cry. (Psalm 40:1)

> If God is for us, who can be against us? He who did not spare his own Son, but gave him up for us all—how will he not also, along with him, graciously give us all things? (Romans 8:31–32)

The LORD is close to the brokenhearted and saves those who are crushed in spirit. (Psalm 34:18)

"If you believe, you will receive whatever you ask for in prayer." (Matthew 21:22)

Considering the season of prayer you're presently in, which of the above promises is most meaningful to you, and why?

8. Bill mentioned that one of his key takeaways from his deep dive into Scripture was discovering that God has a "basic inclination toward kindness." What does it look like to be *inclined toward kindness*? Does this description mesh with your view of God? Explain why or why not to your group.

9. How does God's expectation that his children will come to him and relate with him in prayer itself reflect a posture of kindness toward us?

There was once a judge in some city who never gave God a thought and cared nothing for people. A widow in that city kept after him: "My rights are being violated. Protect me!"

He never gave her the time of day. But after this went on and on he said to himself, "I care nothing what God thinks, even less what people think. But because this widow won't quit badgering me, I'd better do something and see that she gets justice—otherwise I'm going to end up beaten black-and-blue by her pounding."

Luke 18:2–5 MSG

10. Review the story of the persistent widow, located above. How would you characterize your usual posture before God, as it pertains to prayer? Note your answer by placing an X on the scale below, and then explain the reasons for your response to your group.

A Bother
I feel like I have to pester God in order to get his attention.

A Beloved Child
I feel accepted and adored as I approach God in prayer.

11. As Bill mentioned, the biblical story of the persistent widow is often misinterpreted based on how we *really do see God.* Why do you suppose it is easier for many Christ followers to perceive God as an unjust judge who is distant and indifferent than as a loving Father who is near and attentive to our every need?

12. Bill explained that his goal in studying prayer more than two decades ago was not merely *agreeing* with the doctrine of God's omnipotence, but rather *owning* it. What would shift in your attitude or actions if you were to "own" the idea that God really is able to hear you and that he really is powerful enough to help you when you reach out?

> The reality is that our God is good. It's in his nature to be good; it's who he is—a *giving* God, a *blessing* God, an *encouraging* God, a *nurturing* God, an *empowering* God, a *loving* God. This is the God who willingly waits for your call.

PRACTICING PRAYER

Consider wrapping up your group discussion by praying through one or more of the three key concepts addressed during this session. Sample prayer-starters follow.

- **Prayer matters—it always has, and it always will.**
  - *Father, thank you for accomplishing great things throughout history, such as . . .*
  - *Thank you for accomplishing great things in my life, such as . . .*
  - *I know prayer matters, because . . .*
- **God is willing to hear us when we call.**
  - *Thank you for opening your ears to the call and cry of your people and specifically for hearing my prayer today for . . .*
  - *I am grateful for the direct line of communication to you because . . .*
  - *I'm thankful that I can turn to prayer whenever I'm feeling . . .*

- **God, alone, is able to meet our every need.**
  - *Thank you for supplying* _____ *when I'm feeling*
    _____ . . .
  - *Thank you for being* _____ *when I am*
    _____ . . .
  - *Thank you for the gift of prayer, the means for realizing*
    _____ *when I'm experiencing* _____ . . .

BILL'S CHALLENGE
OWNING IT

Look back at the verses quoted in question 7 and select one that you can claim as your own personal promise from God every day of this week. You'll come back to this promise during this session's "On Your Own" segment, but for now, write it in the space below, as a first step in "owning" the doctrine that your heavenly Father loves to hear from you—and to meet pressing needs on your behalf.

The promise I will claim:

_____

_____

_____

_____

_____

_____

_____

_____

_____

_____

_____

SESSION ONE:
ON YOUR OWN

This "On Your Own" section is intended to help you incorporate the video content and group discussion material into your daily life. The three segments—*Journal It*, *Study It*, and *Pray It*—may be completed all at once, or spread out over the days between your group meetings.

JOURNAL IT

Set aside time before your group meets for session 2 to reflect on the questions that follow. You'll find two notes pages for journaling at the end of the session.

- Am I satisfied with the particular "prayer era" I'm in right now? If so, have I thanked God for the open line of communication I enjoy? If not, have I asked him to help me reinvent my prayer life? What would such a reinvention look like?
- What do my recent *practices surrounding prayer* reveal about the *depth of my belief* that God is willing to hear me, and that he is able to help me when I'm in need?
- What current challenge—a strained relationship, a financial hardship, a disheartening set of circumstances—could I devote to prayer this week, instead of worrying about it, trying to control it, or—worse yet—denying that it exists? What would it look like for me to *persist in prayer* on this issue, in the same way that the widow in Luke 18 persisted?

It is hard for God to release his power in your life when you put your hands in your pockets and say, "Thanks, but no thanks. I can handle things on my own."

STUDY IT

Read the story of how Moses' prayer habits affected Joshua's ability to successfully fight the Amalekite army, found in Exodus 17:8–13 (below). Then, answer the questions that follow.

> The Amalekites came and attacked the Israelites at Rephidim. Moses said to Joshua, "Choose some of our men and go out to fight the Amalekites. Tomorrow I will stand on top of the hill with the staff of God in my hands."
>
> So Joshua fought the Amalekites as Moses had ordered, and Moses, Aaron and Hur went to the top of the hill. As long as Moses held up his hands, the Israelites were winning, but whenever he lowered his hands, the Amalekites were winning. When Moses' hands grew tired, they took a stone and put it under him and he sat on it. Aaron and Hur held his hands up—one on one side, one on the other—so that his hands remained steady till sunset. So Joshua overcame the Amalekite army with the sword.
>
> *Exodus 17:8–13*

1. In *Too Busy Not to Pray*, Bill writes, "Moses discovered that day that God's prevailing power is released through prayer. When I began praying in earnest, I also concluded that if I am willing to invite God to involve himself in my practical challenges, I will experience his prevailing power—in my home, in my relationships, in my church, in my leadership roles, wherever it is most needed." In what area of life do you most need a supernatural release of God's prevailing power today?

2. Regarding this particular issue or situation, have you been a "pocket stuffer" who, spiritually speaking, has kept your hands tucked in, or a "prayer warrior" who has unabashedly raised your hands to heaven and cried out to God?

3. What fears or insecurities typically keep you from praying with greater faithfulness or fervency about issues that are important in your life?

PRAY IT

Think back on the promise of Scripture you wished to claim as your own this week, found in the section titled "Bill's Challenge." In the space below, write out a prayer of gratitude to God for this promise, noting why this particular promise is pertinent in your life right now, and how God is using it to mature you in Christ.

SESSION ONE: NOTES

_____

_____

_____

_____

_____

_____

_____

_____

_____

_____

_____

_____

_____

_____

_____

_____

_____

_____

_____

_____

_____

_____

_____

_____

_____

_____

_____

_____

OUR PART OF THE DEAL

Our spirits, like our physical bodies, have requirements for healthy growth, and we "stay in shape" spiritually by praying like Jesus prayed. Throughout the course of his earthly ministry, we find him praying regularly, privately, sincerely, and specifically, and when we uphold habits such as these, our prayer lives see great gains. God's part of the prayer equation is being willing and able to hear and respond to our prayers; being faithful to certain prayer disciplines is our part of the deal.

SUGGESTED READING

Prior to meeting with your group to discuss session 2, read the following chapters of the book *Too Busy Not to Pray* (2008 edition):

Chapter 4, "Heart-Building Habits"
Chapter 5, "Praying Like Jesus"
Chapter 6, "A Pattern for Prayer"
Chapter 7, "Mountain-Moving Prayer"

INTRODUCTION

A woman is weary and out of sorts but decides to go to her office Christmas party anyway. That evening, she happens to meet the brother of her company's managing director, whom she winds up marrying and with whom she celebrates ten, then twenty, then thirty (and still counting!) years of life and joy together.

A couple decides to go to church on a Sunday morning, despite the fact that they slept through their alarm, barely had time to choke down breakfast, and are feeling scattered and rushed. Ninety minutes later, they see their neighbor—the one they've invested many months of spiritual dialogue and friendship in—walk forward and surrender his life to Jesus Christ.

An out-of-work construction guy drives across town on a Saturday morning to help his buddy move into a new home and discovers that his friend's soon-to-be neighbor is a general contractor looking for some help for a project he's just agreed to do.

A teenager drags his feet on the morning of the volunteer opportunity his mom so kindly volunteered him for but shows up at the food bank anyway, only to realize his favorite athlete is making an appearance that day as well.

The moral of these and countless other similar stories is this: *sometimes it pays just to show up.*

True, sometimes we don't feel like praying. Sometimes we don't know what to say. Sometimes we question whether we're ever really heard. But in the *showing up*—in the consistent, faithful, disciplined showing up—we see circumstances shift. We see our faith expanded. We see our loving Father *also* show up to move us, to mature us, to gently mold our lives.

Certainly, God has a role to play, as it pertains to prayer. Scripture tells us that he is faithful to do whatever we ask him to do (John 14:14); to give us the desires of our heart (Psalm 37:4); to answer us and tell us great and unknowable things we do not know (Jeremiah 33:3); to deliver us from our troubles (Psalm 50:15); and to be with us and accomplish whatever it is we need done (Matthew 18:19).

But there is more to the prayer equation than God's part of the deal; you and I *also* have a role to play.

In the same five verses, we read that we, as the pray-ers, must *make our requests known* in Jesus' name; must *delight ourselves in the Lord*; must first *call out to God*; must *reach out to God* on our day of trouble; and must *gather with other believers* in Jesus' name, to agree on what we'd like done.

These and scores of other verses prove the point I'm trying to make: Every prayer promise God delivers in Scripture is kept only as *we show up in prayer*.

CONVERSATION STARTER

Describe for your group a time when you have persisted in getting something you really wanted—a job promotion, your dream house, a date with someone you just *knew* was right for you, a live voice on the other end of a customer-service call, a fair shake from the IRS.

What motivated you to keep "showing up" with such irrepressible tenacity? How did things work out?

VIDEO NOTES

As you watch the video for session 2, use the following outline to record anything that stands out to you.

The importance of showing up

Pray consistently

Pray privately

Pray sincerely

Pray specifically

Persistence pays

The ACTS framework

VIDEO DISCUSSION AND BIBLE STUDY

1. Bill talked about family dinners he has enjoyed over the years, and how humbling for him it is to realize that all he has to do to receive love and laughter and memories to last a lifetime is simply *to show up*. How does this concept of "just showing up" relate to our role in prayer?

PRAY REGULARLY

2. In Matthew 6:6, Jesus gave instructions to his disciples (both then and now) on the importance and practice of prayer, beginning with an overriding assumption: "But *when* you pray ..." he says, meaning that he believes his followers will, in fact, carve out time to pray. Would you say that *regular prayer* is a given in your life these days, or are you a little less reliable than that? Select an option below and then explain the context for your answer to your group.

☐ "Prayer? Well, I have good intentions, but ..."

☐ "I get my mind, heart, and body settled to pray almost every day, but somehow, life interrupts me, and I rarely *actually* pray."

☐ "Prayer is a key part of my life. I don't pray as often as I'd like, but it's definitely a priority."

☐ "For me, prayer is like oxygen; I breathe it in throughout the day, every day."

When we make a habit of prayer, we stay consistently tuned to God's presence and open to receive his blessings.

3. On the grid that follows, list three or four things you tend to find time to do with impressive regularity, such as exercising, reading books to your children, or meeting weekly for coffee with a close friend. What motivates you to keep your commitment to each? An example is provided.

INVOLVEMENTS I DON'T MISS	
What It Is	**What Motivates Me to Stick with It**
Ex.: Exercising	Gives me energy; keeps me from tanking emotionally; helps me fit into my clothes; is a way to spend time with my spouse, since we both enjoy it.

4. When you make time to pray, what would you say is your primary motivation for doing so? In other words, what is the real reason that you pray?

Your prayer room, even if it is a laundry room in the basement, becomes to you what the Garden of Gethsemane became to Jesus — a holy place, the place where God meets with you.

PRAY PRIVATELY

5. Regarding privacy in prayer, Bill mentioned his "prayer cave" experience, where his good intentions for creating a sacred space to commune with God didn't pan out exactly as he had hoped. In what ways can you relate to wanting to spend time in private prayer but having your grand plans thwarted by the practical realities of life?

6. For most of us, privacy is a tough thing to come by. Whether at home, at work, at the gym, or even at church, we tend to be surrounded by people — *lots* of people. Given this reality, the idea of holing away to spend time with God can seem an unattainable dream. How have you learned to counterbalance a "heavily peopled" life? Where do you go to be out of reach and out of touch — if only for a few moments? In a similar vein, how have *proximity* and *pleasantness*, as Bill mentioned, factored into your personal prayer practices?

7. Certainly there is value in corporate prayer; Jesus himself participated in group prayers and encouraged his followers to do the same. But equally important is *private* prayer. What beneficial insights have you gained about yourself and/or about God when you've been faithful to engage in private prayer?

Certain phrases sound so appropriate, so spiritual, so pious, that many people learn to string them together and call that a prayer.

PRAY SINCERELY

8. In describing the dangers of praying insincerely, Bill mentioned four common pitfalls. Which pitfall noted below are you most likely to fall into? Share with your group the influences or experiences that may factor into your inclination.

☐ Praying platitudes or clichés—for example, sitting down to a greasy, fat-laden nutritional nightmare and asking God to "bless this food to the nourishment of our bodies."

☐ Praying jargon or nonsense—for example, asking an omni-present God to "be with us today."

☐ Praying on auto-pilot—for example, passively talking to God about the weather instead of boldly making your real requests known.

☐ Parroting other people's prayers—for example, piling up impressive phrases you've heard others pray, even when such sentiments don't reflect your heart's honest desires.

9. How do your personal observations and experiences either support or challenge Bill's assertion that the two groups of people who tend to pray *most sincerely* are brand-new believers and very mature believers?

> Don't fret or worry. Instead of worrying, pray. Let petitions and praises shape your worries into prayers, letting God know your concerns. Before you know it, a sense of God's wholeness, everything coming together for good, will come and settle you down. It's wonderful what happens when Christ displaces worry at the center of your life.
>
> *Philippians 4:6–7 MSG*

PRAY SPECIFICALLY

10. Regarding the concept of *praying specifically*, we are invited to let our requests—our *specific* requests—be made known to the Father. Read Philippians 4:6–7 above, and then discuss with your group why a sovereign, omniscient God solicits this type of specificity from his children.

11. Bill told the story of standing at his son's friend's bedside recently and boldly asking God to wake Alex from his comatose state and to grant the young man supernatural restoration. When have you been surprised by the results of praying a bold prayer?

12. What is one bold prayer request you are compelled to make known to God today? How does the invitation stated in Hebrews 4:14–16 (below) strengthen your resolve to do so?

> Now that we know what we have—Jesus, this great High Priest with ready access to God—let's not let it slip through our fingers. We don't have a priest who is out of touch with our reality. He's been through weakness and testing, experienced it all—all but the sin. So let's walk right up to him and get what he is so ready to give. Take the mercy, accept the help.
>
> *Hebrews 4:14–16 MSG*

PRACTICING PRAYER

Before ending your time together, consider making the "bold requests" of God that you, as a group, noted in response to question 12.

In keeping with the ACTS framework Bill mentioned, you might make them as part of the "supplications" you offer, after first *adoring* God, *confessing* your sin, and speaking *thanks* for God's goodness in your lives.

> I can write about prayer, and you can read about prayer. But sooner or later you have to fall to your knees and just plain pray.

BILL'S CHALLENGE
AVOIDING THE "PLEASE, GOD" TRAP

In *Too Busy Not to Pray*, Bill writes, "Without a routine for prayer, we inevitably fall into the 'Please, God' trap: 'Please, God, give me. Please, God, help me. Please, God, cover me. Please, God, take care of me.'" The prayer routine Bill finds most helpful—and the way he stays out of the "Please, God" trap!—is based on the acronym ACTS: first adoring God, then confessing sin, then offering thanksgiving for blessings in his life, and finally making his heartfelt requests known.

Before you meet with your group for session 3, take a few moments each day to pray through the ACTS framework, with emphasis on the "bold request" you noted at the end of this session's group time. Consider jotting down salient points from your daily prayers on the notes pages. An example of how to work through the four ACTS categories in light of a single, bold prayer request follows.

Ex.: *Father, please bring home my drug-addicted runaway son.*

A » ADORATION

Thank you, Father, for the gift of family, and specifically for placing my son in ours. Thank you for your heart of compassion toward me, even as I walk through this dark and desperate season. You know what it's like to have a son; you know what it's like to care this much. I praise you because despite my weakness, you are strong; despite my frustrations, you are calm; despite my anger, you are forgiving; despite my pain, you are perfect comfort; despite my feeble footing, you stand steady and sure. You are God, and you are good. All the time, you are good.

C » CONFESSION

I confess to you my fear today—that my kid is gone forever, that my family will never be the same, that our friends will blame us for his behavior, that I'll never have a restful night's sleep again. I know that fear like this is not from you. I claim your forgiveness—and your peace—right now.

T » THANKSGIVING
I'm thankful that you still hear my prayers, and that you are capable of working a miracle in our lives. Your ability to somehow bring beauty from these ashes is my only hope right now.

S » SUPPLICATION
Father, please bring home my son! That is my heart's desire. Please heal our family and give us a massive influx of wisdom and grace as we climb out of this dark pit. I pray, believing you will protect my boy while he is away from us, believing you will spare his life from overdose, believing you will whisper or shout his name so that he'll come to his senses soon.

SESSION TWO:
ON YOUR OWN

This "On Your Own" section is intended to help you incorporate the video content and group discussion material into your daily life. The three segments—*Journal It*, *Study It*, and *Pray It*—may be completed all at once, or spread out over the days between your group meetings.

JOURNAL IT

Set aside time before your group meets for session 3 to reflect on the questions that follow. You'll find two notes pages for journaling at the end of the session.

- If I were to put words to my current prayer practices, how would I describe them?
- Do I really believe something important—*supernatural*, even—could happen to shift my perspective or my particular circumstances if I were simply to "show up" for prayer in a more regular, private, sincere, and specific manner? What are my honest thoughts about the usefulness of prayer, as it relates to the tougher stuff I'm walking through?
- What type of commitment am I prepared to make to God, regarding prizing the priority of prayer?

> As you walk with God, your faith will grow, your confidence will increase, and your prayers will have real power.

STUDY IT

Read the story of the Hebrew patriarch Jacob wrestling with God, found in Genesis 32:22–32 (next page). Then, answer the questions that follow.

That night Jacob got up and took his two wives, his two female servants and his eleven sons and crossed the ford of the Jabbok. After he had sent them across the stream, he sent over all his possessions. So Jacob was left alone, and a man wrestled with him till daybreak. When the man saw that he could not overpower him, he touched the socket of Jacob's hip so that his hip was wrenched as he wrestled with the man. Then the man said, "Let me go, for it is daybreak."

But Jacob replied, "I will not let you go unless you bless me."

The man asked him, "What is your name?"

"Jacob," he answered.

Then the man said, "Your name will no longer be Jacob, but Israel, because you have struggled with God and with humans and have over-come."

Jacob said, "Please tell me your name."

But he replied, "Why do you ask my name?" Then he blessed him there.

So Jacob called the place Peniel, saying, "It is because I saw God face to face, and yet my life was spared."

The sun rose above him as he passed Peniel, and he was limping because of his hip. Therefore to this day the Israelites do not eat the tendon attached to the socket of the hip, because the socket of Jacob's hip was touched near the tendon.

Genesis 32:22–32

1. Why do you suppose God rewarded a verbal demand and even a *wrestling match* from one of his own? What does God's response here reveal to you about his nature?

2. Toward the end of this week's session, Bill said that as God's children, we never should be afraid to "go to the mat" with God, as Jacob did, on certain issues that are near and dear to our hearts. What divine answers to prayer have you received only by wrestling in this way with God?

3. Jacob eventually received the blessing from God he desired, but he also received a permanent limp as a result of the encounter. If you knew that receiving your desired answer to prayer would require that you lived the rest of your life with a limp of some sort—be it physical, emotional, spiritual, relational, financial, or otherwise—would you still pursue the blessing you seek? Describe your thoughts below.

PRAY IT

Consider taking "Bill's Challenge" to lift up the value of structured prayer as you bring your "bold request" before God. Use either the ACTS framework he described or another structure that better resonates with you. The structure itself is not as important as upholding your part of the deal in the divine dialogue known as prayer. Write your prayer here if you like.

Session Two: Notes

WHEN PRAYER FEELS HARD

In the same way that we know what makes prayer easier—praying regularly, praying privately, praying sincerely, and praying specifically—we also know what makes prayer feel hard. Prayerlessness. Relational conflict. Selfishness. Unconfessed sin. Lack of compassion or persistence or faith. The list could go on, but you get the idea: when we go our way instead of God's way, our prayer muscles get flabby and weak. As a result, prayer feels hard.

SUGGESTED READING

Prior to meeting with your group to discuss session 3, read the following chapters of the book *Too Busy Not to Pray* (2008 edition):

Chapter 8, "The Hurt of Unanswered Prayer"
Chapter 9, "Prayer Busters"
Chapter 10, "Cooling Off on Prayer"
Chapter 11, "Slowing Down to Pray"
Chapter 12, "The Importance of Listening"

INTRODUCTION

A quick scan of the horizon in our families, in our neighborhoods, in our businesses and churches, in our country, and around the globe plainly reveals that all is not as it should be here on planet Earth. Loving families watch their wayward kids ditch wisdom and pursue drug addiction instead. Spouses spend an inordinate amount of time and money helping their soul mates battle cancer, MS, Parkinson's, and more, only to watch those loved ones lose the fight. Caring people drop everything to come to the aid of neighbors in crisis, but the help proves too little, too late.

We see the not-right trend on the horizon of our hearts as well. A wrong done to us never gets made right. A spirit of discouragement never seems to lift. A deep-seated desire just never gets met. And it's not for lack of fervent prayer that these realities are true; they are true *in spite of* our prayers.

We pray. We pray *a lot*. We pray boldly. We pray regularly. We pray privately. We pray sincerely. We pray specifically. We do everything we are supposed to do! And yet sometimes, what God chooses to do in response is ... nothing.

There are times when prayer feels easy—the connection is clear, the motivations are pure, the words are flowing, the answers are quick. And then there are times when it's hard. We beat our heads against the brick wall of our situation, begging God to *please* knock it down. If only he'd remove even one brick. If only we could see a sliver of light—of hope—peeking through. If only we knew that our prayers here mattered, that they'd somehow make a difference in the end.

Thankfully, Scripture addresses this issue of what to do when prayer feels hard. There are *reasons* we can learn to spot, and there are *responses* we can learn to give.

CONVERSATION STARTER

Country superstar Garth Brooks once sang of thanking God for unanswered prayer, because later in life he realized that some of the things he'd prayed for along the way would have utterly destroyed him, had God chosen to dole out yeses left and right. Describe to your group one "unanswered prayer" you're grateful for, now that you have the benefit of hindsight.

VIDEO NOTES

As you watch the video for session 3, use the following outline to record anything that stands out to you.

Unanswered prayer is sometimes a mystery

Gut-check question 1: *Have I actually prayed regularly and fervently about this matter?*

Gut-check question 2: *Am I harboring any unconfessed sin?*

Gut-check question 3: *Am I aware of any unresolved relational conflict in my life?*

Gut-check question 4: *Are my prayer requests just plain selfish?*

Gut-check question 5: *Does my heart beat for the poor?*

Gut-check question 6: *Do I lack faith?*

What are you waiting for?

VIDEO DISCUSSION AND BIBLE STUDY
PRAYERLESSNESS

1. The first reason Bill cited for unanswered prayer is simple *prayerlessness*—we fail to receive an answer from God because we fail to persist in prayer. Read James 5:13–16 below and then discuss with your group the following question: How does this passage support or contradict Bill's assertion that a wholehearted prayer life is more honoring to God than a series of hit-or-miss prayers?

> Is anyone among you in trouble? Let them pray. Is anyone happy? Let them sing songs of praise. Is anyone among you sick? Let them call the elders of the church to pray over them and anoint them with oil in the name of the Lord. And the prayer offered in faith will make the sick person well; the Lord will raise them up. If they have sinned, they will be forgiven. Therefore confess your sins to each other and pray for each other so that you may be healed. The prayer of a righteous person is powerful and effective.
>
> *James 5:13–16*

2. In your own prayer life, how do you stave off the tendency toward prayerlessness? What postures or practices have you found to be most useful?

UNCONFESSED SIN

3. The second reason cited for unanswered prayer is *unconfessed sin*. Read Isaiah 59:1−2 below and then discuss with your group why it is that our sin necessarily causes separation between God and us in prayer.

> Surely the arm of the LORD is not too short to save, nor his ear too dull to hear. But your iniquities have separated you from your God; your sins have hidden his face from you, so that he will not hear.
>
> *Isaiah 59:1−2*

4. There are three parts to honest confession: *acknowledgment, agreement*, and *avoidance*. First, you recognize a decision you've made or an action you've taken as sin; next, you agree with God that it represents less than his best for your life; and finally, you turn from that course and begin again in a direction that honors God. While these labels may be new to you, the process is probably one you've experienced. When have you worked through these three steps, and what gains did you realize in your prayer life as a result?

UNRESOLVED RELATIONAL CONFLICT

5. A third reason for unanswered prayer is *unresolved relational conflict*. After reading Matthew 5:23–24 (below), note on the grid that follows the character traits you assume are necessary for a person to possess in order to follow Jesus' injunction, and why. Discuss your thoughts with your group.

> Therefore, if you are offering your gift at the altar and there remember that your brother or sister has something against you, leave your gift there in front of the altar. First go and be reconciled to them; then come and offer your gift.
>
> *Matthew 5:23–24*

KEYS TO RESOLVING RELATIONAL CONFLICT

Character Trait Needed	Why It's Needed

6. Which of the traits you noted on the grid in question 5 do you wish you had more of, and why?

7. Romans 12:18 says that as far as it depends on us, we should live at peace with all people. There are both an action suggested and an allowance offered here: we are to *strive at all times for peace* (the action), but we are to recognize that *we may not be able to achieve it* in every situation (the allowance). How did Jesus' ministry while on planet Earth reflect this tension? How have you personally experienced it?

8. What does being "at peace" with people have to do with experiencing a profitable prayer life?

SELFISHNESS AND A HEART THAT DOESN'T BEAT FOR THE POOR

9. The fourth and fifth items on Bill's unanswered-prayer checklist are inextricably linked: *selfishness* and *a heart that doesn't beat for the poor.* Isaiah 58:6–14 offers a treasure trove of insights from God regarding how to live selflessly. Which expectation listed in the passage that follows do you find most convicting, and why? On the flip side of the coin, which, if any, do you tend to uphold?

This is the kind of fast day I'm after: to break the chains of injustice, get rid of exploitation in the workplace, free the oppressed, cancel debts. What I'm interested in seeing you do is: sharing your food with the hungry, inviting the homeless poor into your homes, putting clothes on the shivering ill-clad, being available to your own families. Do this and the lights will turn on, and your lives will turn around at once. Your righteousness will pave your way. The GOD of glory will secure your passage. Then when you pray, GOD will answer. You'll call out for help and I'll say, "Here I am."

If you get rid of unfair practices, quit blaming victims, quit gossiping about other people's sins, if you are generous with the hungry and start giving yourselves to the down-and-out, your lives will begin to glow in the darkness, your shadowed lives will be bathed in sunlight. I will always show you where to go. I'll give you a full life in the emptiest of places—firm muscles, strong bones.

You'll be like a well-watered garden, a gurgling spring that never runs dry. You'll use the old rubble of past lives to build anew, rebuild the foundations from out of your past. You'll be known as those who can fix anything, restore old ruins, rebuild and renovate, make the community livable again.

If you watch your step on the Sabbath and don't use my holy day for personal advantage, if you treat the Sabbath as a day of joy, GOD's holy day as a celebration, if you honor it by refusing "business as usual," making money, running here and there—then you'll be free to enjoy GOD!

Oh, I'll make you ride high and soar above it all. I'll make you feast on the inheritance of your ancestor Jacob.

Isaiah 58:6–14 MSG

10. When have you personally known some of the benefits of self-lessness described in this passage? Why do you suppose God established such a strong connection between our commitment to selfless living and our receiving answers in prayer?

INADEQUATE FAITH

11. Bill's sixth and final reason for unanswered prayer is *inadequate faith.* In order to refill our faith tank when it's low, Bill suggested reviewing God's faithfulness in our life. How might

focusing on God's past faithfulness strengthen our belief that he'll come through for us in future days?

WHEN PRAYER FEELS HARD FOR YOU

12. Of the six reasons Bill cited for prayer feeling hard (see below), which do you most often experience? What factors do you suppose are to blame?

☐ Prayerlessness

☐ Unconfessed sin

☐ Unresolved relational conflict

☐ Selfishness

☐ A heart that doesn't beat for the poor

☐ Inadequate faith

PRACTICING PRAYER

We all struggle in prayer from time to time. Based on your group's answers to question 12, consider spending a few moments in prayer before you dismiss. Using the verses below as springboards, ask God to help each person in your group overcome the main obstacle to prayer he or she is facing today.

1. *Regarding breaking free from the hindrance of prayerlessness...*

   "Let us then approach God's throne of grace with confidence, so that we may receive mercy and find grace to help us in our time of need" (Hebrews 4:16).

2. *Regarding breaking free from the hindrance of unconfessed sin...*

   "The LORD is merciful and gracious, slow to anger, and abounding in mercy. He will not always strive with us, nor will

He keep His anger forever. He has not dealt with us according to our sins, nor punished us according to our iniquities. For as the heavens are high above the earth, so great is His mercy toward those who fear Him; as far as the east is from the west, so far has He removed our transgressions from us" (Psalm 103:8–12 NKJV).

3. **Regarding breaking free from the hindrance of unresolved relational conflict . . .**

   "The LORD is a shelter for the oppressed, a refuge in times of trouble. Those who know your name trust in you, for you, O LORD, do not abandon those who search for you" (Psalm 9:9–10 NLT).

-and-

   "Depend on the LORD and his strength; always go to him for help" (1 Chronicles 16:11 NCV).

4. **Regarding breaking free from the hindrance of selfishness . . .**

   "Let's take a good look at the way we're living and reorder our lives under GOD. Let's lift our hearts and hands at one and the same time, praying to God in heaven: 'We've been contrary and willful' " (Lamentations 3:40–42 MSG).

5. **Regarding breaking free from the hindrance of a heart that doesn't beat for the poor . . .**

   "Give in to God, come to terms with him and everything will turn out just fine. Let him tell you what to do; take his words to heart. Come back to God Almighty and he'll rebuild your life. Clean house of everything evil. Relax your grip on your money and abandon your gold-plated luxury. God Almighty will be your treasure, more wealth than you can imagine.

   "You'll take delight in God, the Mighty One, and look to him joyfully, boldly. You'll pray to him and he'll listen; he'll help you do what you've promised. You'll decide what you want and it will happen; your life will be bathed in light. To those

who feel low you'll say, 'Chin up! Be brave!' and God will save them. Yes, even the guilty will escape, escape through God's grace in your life" (Job 22:21–30 MSG).

6. ***Regarding breaking free from the hindrance of inadequate faith ...***

"I waited patiently for the LORD; he turned to me and heard my cry. He lifted me out of the slimy pit, out of the mud and mire; he set my feet on a rock and gave me a firm place to stand. He put a new song in my mouth, a hymn of praise to our God. Many will see and fear the LORD and put their trust in him.

"Blessed is the one who trusts in the LORD, who does not look to the proud, to those who turn aside to false gods. Many, LORD my God, are the wonders you have done, the things you planned for us. None can compare with you; were I to speak and tell of your deeds, they would be too many to declare" (Psalm 40:1–5).

BILL'S CHALLENGE
SO-THAT PRAYING

Write down your major requests of God this week, tracking your so-that motivation for each one. You'll find a grid for recording your prayers and purposes in this session's "On Your Own" section.

Before closing your group time, gather insights from the rest of your group about the best way to work through this challenge. Jot down helpful ideas in the space below.

Session Three:
On Your Own

This "On Your Own" section is intended to help you incorporate the video content and group discussion material into your daily life. The three segments—*Journal It*, *Study It*, and *Pray It*—may be completed all at once, or spread out over the days between your group meetings.

Journal It

Set aside time before your group meets for session 4 to reflect on the questions that follow. You'll find two notes pages for journaling at the end of the session.

- After learning about six habits that render a person's prayer life impotent, which areas am I most compelled to take a closer look at—and shore up?
- What would growth in these areas look like? What would it require of me? What promises of God would I need to claim in order to see the process through?
- As it relates to keeping my faith-meter pegged, how would I put words to God's faithfulness in my life thus far, according to the following four key categories: my heritage—both my family tree and my personal history; my habits; my health; and my heart's deepest desires? How can I keep these evidences of his faithfulness top of mind going forward?

> If the truth were known, often you and I are the only obstacles standing in the way of our receiving a desperately needed miracle.

Study It

Read from Isaiah 1:16–20 (next page) God's advice to the nation Israel—and, perhaps closer to home, to anyone who has intentionally or unintentionally cooled off on prayer—and then answer the questions that follow.

> "Wash and make yourselves clean. Take your evil deeds out of my sight; stop doing wrong. Learn to do right; seek justice. Defend the oppressed. Take up the cause of the fatherless; plead the case of the widow.
>
> "Come now, let us settle the matter," says the LORD. "Though your sins are like scarlet, they shall be as white as snow; though they are red as crimson, they shall be like wool. If you are willing and obedient, you will eat the good things of the land; but if you resist and rebel, you will be devoured by the sword."
>
> *Isaiah 1:16–20*

1. Based on this text, what is your role, and what is God's role, in the process of getting your life back on track when you have neglected to go his way?

   Your Role:

   God's Role:

2. How does God's proven faithfulness in his role affect your desire to be faithful in yours?

3. In *Too Busy Not to Pray*, Bill Hybels writes, "I plead with you, do not lose heart. Keep on praying because the Father *does* listen. He hears every prayer we pray, and he cares deeply about everything that affects us. He has *unlimited power* to bring to bear on whatever is causing our concern. True, he doesn't answer every prayer the way we fallible human beings wish he would. But he loves our company, he wants us to endure in prayerfulness and he is eager to do what is best for us." How will you keep from "losing heart" this week, regarding the parts of your prayer life that presently feel hard?

PRAY IT

On the full-page grid that follows, write down three or four major requests of God this week, tracking your so-that motivation for each. An example has been provided.

God says, "I want to guide your life. I know the path that will glorify me and be productive for you, and I want to put you on it."

SO-THAT PRAYING	
My Prayer Request	**My So-That Motivation**
Ex.: Father, please help my husband get the job he's interviewing for tomorrow.	We need the money **so that** we can afford to live. And the insurance **so that** we have coverage if we get sick.

What I learned from tracking my prayer motivations this week:

SESSION THREE: NOTES

PEOPLE
OF PRAYER

People of prayer believe both in the nearness of God and in the immensity of God. They experience his presence consistently, continually, conversationally, and confidently, even as they recognize they're dealing with the omniscient, omnipotent One who created it all. They come before him with boldness, letting their earnest requests be made known. And they wait with happy hearts and souls that know that the same God who put each star in its place longs to answer each prayer that they pray.

SUGGESTED READING

Prior to meeting with your group to discuss session 4, read the following chapters of the book *Too Busy Not to Pray* (2008 edition):

Chapter 13, "How to Hear God's Promptings"
Chapter 14, "What to Do with Promptings"
Chapter 15, "Living in God's Presence"
Chapter 16, "The Needs Around Us"

INTRODUCTION

Talk to anyone who has left a positive mark in a particular field of involvement, and you'll discover a common theme: *success in any endeavor comes only by hard work.* The businessperson who blows out sales quotas quarter after quarter; the parent who implements innovative discipline strategies with his or her kids; the pastor who lifts the sights and the energies of a congregation; the professor who calls the best out of a class of students; the volunteer who somehow is able to rally ever-increasing levels of support around a cause—these people all understand that to produce effective results, passion and persistence are required.

We don't *drift* into becoming sales superstars. We don't *drift* into becoming admirable parents. We don't *drift* into becoming visionary pastors. We don't *drift* into becoming inspiring teachers. We don't *drift* into becoming world-changing activists. No, effectiveness in *any* aspect of life requires us to set our sights, chart our course, and persist until we reach our goal.

There's a very spiritual lesson in all of this, which is that in order to become people of prayer, we must apply the same intention and drive.

Regardless of how pure our motivation is, the simple truth is that you and I can't drift into a lifestyle of prayer. We can't cruise into conversational intimacy with the Almighty. Far from it! We have to doggedly *demand* that prayerfulness will be our way of life. And not just once; we have to choose this way day after day, hour after hour, breath after divinely given breath.

We pray because we know that prayer is what knits our hearts to the heart of our heavenly Father. And we *keep* praying because in those hearts we have determined to be Christ-following people of prayer.

CONVERSATION STARTER

When have you trained for something—such as a new role, a new endeavor, or a competition of some kind—and realized success as a result of your preparation? Was the preparation easier or more difficult than you originally imagined it would be? Was it worth it in the end?

Describe the experience to your group.

VIDEO NOTES

As you watch the video for session 4, use the following outline to record anything that stands out to you.

The truth about people of prayer

Rituals that keep us in "prayer mode"

Jesus' prayer practices

Prayer disciplines that have served Bill well

The impact we could have as people of prayer

"God, here are my hands"

Video Discussion and Bible Study

1. In his opening remarks this session, Bill made the comment that if he were facing emergency surgery, he knows *exactly* who he'd call to ask for prayer on his behalf. What characteristics (besides prayerfulness, of course) define a person of prayer? Do

you think you're considered a "person of prayer" by friends and family members who know you best? Why or why not?

2. When have you felt the "uplift" that being prayed for by someone else can provide? Describe the experience to your group, noting the situation in your life that necessitated prayer, the person (or people) of prayer who interceded on your behalf, and what happened as a result.

When you practice being aware of God's presence, you pick up his signals all through the day. At work, at home, in your car, or wherever you are, you begin to dialogue with the Lord. You share your heart with him and you know he's listening. It has nothing to do with being in a church building or on your knees. It has to do with God's presence in and around you—"Christ in you," Colossians 1:27 says, "the hope of glory."

3. People of prayer practice prayer rituals that help them stay connected to God throughout their day. What prayer rituals have you experimented with along the way, and what benefits have they yielded? Jot down your thoughts on the following grid, and then share a few entries from your list with your group. An example has been provided.

MY PRAYER RITUALS	
The Ritual	**How It Helps**
Ex.: Taking ten seconds every time I get behind the wheel of my car to exhale and to ask for God's protection and peace as I pull out.	Centers my mind, focuses my attention, helps hold me accountable to being a responsible driver instead of a distracted one.

People who truly are interested in hearing from God understand that there is a price to be paid, which usually comes in the form of *disciplined stillness.*

4. How might the practice of prayer rituals lead to a keener ability to detect promptings or "whispers" from God?

5. In chapter 14 of *Too Busy Not to Pray*, Bill notes the following three criteria for determining if a prompting is from God:

- All promptings that come from God are consistent with his Word, the Bible.
- God's promptings are usually consistent with the person he made you to be.
- God's promptings usually involve servanthood.

When have you experienced a significant prompting from God to do (or not do) something, to say (or not say) something? Were you faithful to obey? What happened as a result of your response to God's request? Describe the experience to your group.

> When God tells us to do something, as long as it's within the limits set by Scripture, we don't have to understand it. All we need to do is obey … and then trust God to use our obedience to accomplish his will.

6. In closing this session, Bill said that his heart's desire was that throughout his days and throughout his life, his hands would be *lifted to God in worship*, and that they would be *put to practical use in fixing what is broken in this world*. In your view, how are the two ideas connected?

> Jesus would say throughout his teaching that his followers would be marked by mercy. What would distinguish them from the non-followers is that their hearts would race for people in need. Their hands would wrestle for resources that they could then give away. Their wallets would reflect sacrificial stretching to meet people's needs instead of settling for doling out five-dollar hits here and there. Their minds would work diligently to wrap themselves around the real issues under-resourced people face. "My followers," Jesus would teach, "are going to *fight* for the poor." And based on my experience, this God-enabled fighting spirit shows up only when I am down on my knees.

7. Describe a season of your life when you have experienced this dynamic of your hands being lifted in worship and, as a result, being outstretched in service.

8. Read the lyrics of Aaron Niequist's song "Here Are My Hands" that follow. What would it look like for you to live out the words "Your kingdom come, my kingdom go" with passion and with persistence? How might prayerfulness as a lifestyle contribute to such a goal?

HERE ARE MY HANDS
Aaron Niequest

So here are my hands
They're small
Here are my hands
They're small and trembling
Here are my arms
They're weak
Here are my arms
They're weak but willing

Here are my eyes
They burn with memories
Here are my eyes
They're teared and tired
Here are my feet

cont.

They're slow
They're stumbling to you now

God I know there's still so much I just don't know
God I believe your kingdom can still be built in me
So here is my heart
Here is my soul
Take me in part
Take me in whole
I want to be whole

Here are my hands, they're small
Here are my hands, they're small and trembling
Here are my dreams
They're well protected
So please be gentle now

God I know there's still so much I just don't know
God I believe your kingdom can still be built on me
So here is my heart
Here is my soul
Your kingdom come
My kingdom go

I'm letting it go
I'm letting it go
I'm letting it go

Get before God. Ask him to give you his eyes to see, his ears to hear, his mind to think wisely. Ask him to usher you into your God-designed era for helping to fix all that's wrong in this very wrong world. He will be faithful to answer you and to guide you. He will provide peace so that you can live in the midst of darkness with unquenchable light. And he will provide power so that your life will count between now and an eternity spent by his side.

PRACTICING PRAYER

Before ending your time together, consider praying as a group with hands open and palms turned upward. Ask God to provide divine wisdom for all members of your group to know the attitudes and actions that will invite his kingdom to come and allow their kingdom to go.

Ask him to make you *people of prayer*.

BILL'S CHALLENGE
"HERE ARE MY HANDS"

Let your hands point you to prayer this week; whatever you put your hands to, invite God's presence and power there. For example, as you open the refrigerator door, pray a prayer of thanksgiving for food to eat in a hungry world. As you turn on the kitchen faucet, pray a prayer of acknowledgment that countless millions of people around the globe lack clean drinking water. As you flip on light switches, pray a prayer of surrender, that you would be light in your corner of the world.

As you slip behind the wheel of your vehicle, pray for safety as you go. As you tie your shoes or button your shirt, pray that you'll be clothed throughout your day in righteousness. As you wave to your neighbor, pray for the needs you're aware of—or, if you don't yet have a relationship with him or her, pray for an open door toward that end. As you tuck in your kids at night, pray peace over their sleep and protection over their hearts. As you hug a loved one, pray blessings on his or her life.

Whatever your hands find to do, let God's presence and power come there too. And at the close of each day, fill in that day's grid on the pages that follow as a way to record your experience.

"HERE ARE MY HANDS" LOG

Day/Date: _____

What I Put My Hands To	The Prayer I Was Prompted to Pray

Day/Date: _____

What I Put My Hands To	The Prayer I Was Prompted to Pray

"HERE ARE MY HANDS" LOG

Day/Date:_____

What I Put My Hands To	The Prayer I Was Prompted to Pray

Day/Date:_____

What I Put My Hands To	The Prayer I Was Prompted to Pray

"Here Are My Hands" Log

Day/Date:_____

What I Put My Hands To	The Prayer I Was Prompted to Pray

Day/Date:_____

What I Put My Hands To	The Prayer I Was Prompted to Pray

"HERE ARE MY HANDS" LOG

Day/Date: _____

What I Put My Hands To	The Prayer I Was Prompted to Pray

SESSION FOUR:
ON YOUR OWN

This "On Your Own" section is intended to help you incorporate the video content and group discussion material into your daily life. The three segments—*Journal It*, *Study It*, and *Pray It*—may be completed all at once, or spread out over the coming days.

JOURNAL IT

Set aside time following your final group discussion to reflect on the questions that follow. You'll find two notes pages for journaling at the end of the session.

- So, who *would* I call if I were facing emergency surgery and needed prayer?
- Am I known in my circle of influence as a person of prayer? If so, what useful practices should I persist in? If not, what changes might I make—such as reading a helpful book, enlisting the accountability of a trusted and prayerful friend, or memorizing a compelling portion of Scripture—to become this type of person?
- Do my daily patterns reflect a reliance on "prayer rituals" as a means of staying connected to God? Which new rituals am I interested in trying? What benefit(s) do I hope to see?
- How might an increased emphasis on prayerfulness aid my role as a friend, a parent, a spouse, an employee, a neighbor,

Your heavenly Friend always listens. He freely communicates with you without barriers. When he expresses affection, he means it. He is patient with your immaturity, forgives you when you wrong him, and stays committed to you even when you ignore him for long periods of time. He is always faithful.

or a global citizen? What do I suspect might be accomplished by prayer in these relationships that wouldn't be accomplished any other way?

STUDY IT

Read Luke 12:48 below and then answer the questions that follow.

From everyone who has been given much, much will be demanded; and from the one who has been entrusted with much, much more will be asked.

Luke 12:48

1. Why do you suppose it is easier for people of prayer to stay clear on the fact that because they have been given much, much will be required of them as they walk with Christ?

2. How would you describe the "much" that you have been given by God?

3. How would you describe the "much" that God may be asking you to relinquish for the purposes of meeting other people's needs?

4. What role does prayer play in forging an attitude of gratitude for the *much* you've been given, and in tenderizing your heart as you present to God the *much* that he requires?

PRAY IT

Ask God for eyes that see the lavish provision he has made in your life, and for hands that are willing to pass those blessings along to people in need.

Sure, you can look forward to eternal life in heaven. But between now and then, your earthly life can actually *matter*.

SESSION FOUR: NOTES

TIPS FOR
GROUPS

Leading a small group through this four-session study is a straight-forward process. Simply determine the composition of your group—for instance, fellow churchgoers, neighbors, business associates, friends, family members—and follow the instructions below. Your thoughtful preparation will ensure a meaningful experience for all.

BEFORE YOU MEET

Prior to your first group meeting, establish a day and time for each of the four sessions that will ensure maximum attendance. Be sure to obtain and distribute materials (see next page) prior to convening to discuss session 1, and encourage participants to read chapters 1–3 of the book *Too Busy Not to Pray* **before** that meeting. As group leader, you may wish to review the video and study guide content for session 1 prior to working through the material in full group.

Each group member should have the following materials prior to meeting for session 1:

- *Too Busy Not to Pray*, by Bill Hybels (2008 edition)
- *Too Busy Not to Pray Study Guide*
- Bible

MAXIMIZING GROUP TIME

Each of the four sessions included in this study has been designed for a 90-minute meeting, which breaks out roughly this way:

1. Conversation Starter . . . . 10 minutes
2. Video . . . . 20 minutes
3. Group Discussion . . . . 50 minutes
4. Group Prayer/Discuss "Bill's Challenge" . . . 10 minutes

If your group only meets for an hour, adjust discussion times accordingly.

As leader, you can help maximize group discussions by scanning the session's material prior to each meeting. Mark the questions you want to be sure to cover, and then come back to additional questions if time permits. Be respectful of your group's time by sticking to agreed-upon start and end times.

Keep group discussions balanced by tempering talkers and drawing out quieter participants. And be sure to be honoring of *all* group members — their spiritual background, their hopes and fears, their experience with the subject matter, and so forth.

Finally, encourage your participants to take time to complete each session's "On Your Own" segment between group meetings in order to personalize what they're learning. If you're able, check in with each member between group meetings to see what questions they have, and to discover how you can be praying for them throughout the study.

A Word about Prayer

As leader of a study on the subject of prayer, *don't forget to pray!* Pray regularly for your group members by name. Pray for each meeting. Pray for transformation to occur. Bring your heartfelt requests to God, and prepare for him to do great things in your midst.

Companion Book Available
from
≈ InterVarsity Press

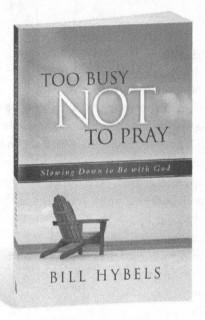

ISBN 978-0-8308-3475-4
PAPERBACK, 198 PAGES

Available in bookstores everywhere

Discounts available on bulk orders
for U.S. addresses only

To order, call 1-800-843-9487

The Power of a Whisper DVD Study

Hearing God, Having the Guts to Respond

Bill Hybels

Join bestselling author and pastor Bill Hybels as he casts vision for what life can look like when directed by divine input from above. In this four-session video-based study (participant's guide also available), your group will learn to navigate life through whispers from God ... whispers that arbitrate key decisions, whispers that rescue you from a dark night of the soul, whispers that spur on growth, whispers that come by way of another person, whispers that open your eyes to the terrible plight people face in this world.

Through this dynamic teaching and group study, you will learn to practice hearing from God, surrender to the voice of God, obey his promptings, and become a more effective kingdom-builder.

Sessions include:

1. The Whisper-Led Life
2. Divine Input for the Day-to-Day
3. Practice, Practice, Practice
4. Wide Open for Good

Available in stores and online!

ZONDERVAN®
.com

Just Walk Across the Room DVD Study

Four Sessions on Simple Steps Pointing People to Faith

Bill Hybels

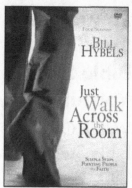

Just Walk Across the Room signals the next era in personal evangelism. Pastor Bill Hybels's firm conviction is that the highest value in personal evangelism is being attuned to and cooperative with the promptings of the Holy Spirit. This means playing only the role one is intended to play—walking when the Spirit says to walk, talking when the Spirit says to talk, and falling silent when the Spirit suggests that you've already said enough.

According to Hybels, the goal for every Christian is to reflect Christ's love and follow his example by taking simple walks across rooms, leaving one's circles of comfort and extending hands of care, compassion, and inclusiveness to people living far from God.

The DVD (participant's guide also available) includes four video sessions that expand on the teaching from Hybels's book of the same name, as well as personal testimonies of lives transformed by the Holy Spirit. Also included are all the sermon and promotional materials needed for churches to successfully launch and sustain a four week whole church campaign.

Sessions include:

1. The Single Greatest Gift
2. Living in 3D
3. The Power of Story
4. Grander Vision Living

Zondervan Small Group Bible Study YouTube Playlist

Watch Over 100 Full Bible Study Sessions for Free

Watch the entire first lesson for many of Zondervan's DVD based Bible studies. No more guessing on the content, instead you get the full video experience by being able to see and evaluate the complete first lesson of each multi-lesson Bible study.

Each video is easy to share with your friends, small group or Bible study. Just hit the 'share' button under the video and send it via email, Facebook, or Twitter.

Watch Bible study sessions from bestselling authors like Bill Hybels, Timothy Keller, Andy Stanley, Anne Graham Lotz , Craig Groeschel, Jim Cymbala, John Ortberg, Lysa TerKeurst, and many more.

Zondervan video-based group Bible studies are available on DVD, and many are available for download. These video Bible studies feature a variety of topics from many authors, and are available wherever small group resources and curriculum are sold.

Watch sessions from bestselling studies including:

- *The Power of a Whisper* by Bill Hybels
- *The Reason for God* by Timothy Keller
- *Guardrails* by Andy Stanley
- *The Christian Atheist* by Craig Groeschel
- *Undaunted* by Christine Caine
- *The Circle Maker* by Mark Batterson

WILLOW CREEK ASSOCIATION

This resource is just one of many ministry tools published in partnership with the Willow Creek Association. Founded in 1992, WCA was created to serve churches and church leaders striving to create environments where those still outside the family of God are welcomed—and can more easily consider God's loving offer of salvation through faith.

These innovative churches and leaders are connected at the deepest level by their all-out dedication to Christ and His Kingdom. Willing to do whatever it required to build churches that help people move along the path toward Christ-centered devotion; they also share a deep desire to encourage all believers at every step of their faith journey, to continue moving toward a fully transformed, Christ-centered life.

Today, more than 10,000 churches from 80 denominations worldwide are formally connected to WCA and each other through WCA Membership. Many thousands more come to WCA for networking, training, and resources.

For more information about the ministry of the
Willow Creek Association, visit: **willowcreek.com**.

Share Your Thoughts

With the Author: Your comments will be forwarded to
the author when you send them to *zauthor@zondervan.com.*

With Zondervan: Submit your review of this book
by writing to *zreview@zondervan.com.*

Free Online Resources at
www.zondervan.com

Zondervan AuthorTracker: Be notified whenever your favorite
authors publish new books, go on tour, or post an update
about what's happening in their lives at www.zondervan.com/
authortracker.

Daily Bible Verses and Devotions: Enrich your life with daily
Bible verses or devotions that help you start every morning
focused on God. Visit www.zondervan.com/newsletters.

Free Email Publications: Sign up for newsletters on Christian
living, academic resources, church ministry, fiction, children's
resources, and more. Visit www.zondervan.com/newsletters.

Zondervan Bible Search: Find and compare Bible passages in
a variety of translations at www.zondervanbiblesearch.com.

Other Benefits: Register to receive online benefits like
coupons and special offers, or to participate in research.